BIBLICAL COURTSHIP

PREPARING YOUNGSTERS FOR MARRIAGE

EVANS FRANCIS

ISBN 979-888555109-0

I dedicate this book with love to my wife, Neha, who has consistently given me more than I ever prayed for. You and I both know prayer works.

Contents

Introduction

In a world where morality is declining and immorality is increasing like never before, I feel an urgent need to help misguided young people avoid several pitfalls on their journeys through life. Hence, I decided to write this life-saving book to guide these youths, some of whom have no one to lead them on the right spiritual path. This happens because many parents are busy trying to meet the demands of work, provide for their families, and offer their children bright futures. As a result, matters about marriage, sex, and life, in general, tend to be left on the back burner.

This book is also a guide to parents who want to help their kids grow morally and spiritually, preparing them for a better future.

My burden to write stems from the discontent I feel with the current world—a world where every wrong thing is accepted as a trophy, a world where newlyweds think twice about whether they should allow a baby to be born.

I pray this book will transform the mindsets and lives of many young people. May God use it to make a difference.

Connect with Evans Francis

WhatsApp: https://wa.me/919960877313

YouTube: www.youtube.com/evansfrancis

Facebook: https://www.facebook.com/evansfrancis831

Instagram: https://www.instagram.com/evansfrancis831

Website: www.evansfrancis.org
     www.evansfrancisbooks.com
     www.christianappdevelopers.com

Email: contact@evansfrancis.org

CHAPTER ONE

What Is Biblical Courtship?

The choices you make in life will determine your blessings and curses. Who you date, court, and marry are significant choices you will make along the way that can play a big role in what your future looks like. Therefore, you must understand what the Bible says about these matters, so you can live according to God's plan.

Biblical courtship exists so people can get married, have children, and create a godly heritage. Interestingly, before God established the church on the earth, He instituted marriage. In fact, from the time Eve came to life, God ordained marriage. It is one of the most sacred institutions created by God Himself. Moreover, it is one of the most important commitments you will make in your life. You and your spouse will be joint-heirs of God's gift of life.

Despite what the world says, we are not called to be in long-term relationships. Rather, we were made for lifelong marriages. If you are not aiming for the ring, what is your reason for courting? Most likely, your destination will be the bed of fornication.

God's way of courting or dating is miles apart from the world's. The world subscribes to one-night stands and shacking up, while God's way is for a man and woman to make intentional advances toward marriage. If you are not ready to be married in the near future, then you are not ready to be in a relationship with someone. Why? You have no goal in mind. Without a goal, you will wander aimlessly and waste each other's time.

Before proceeding, I wish to implore teenagers to respect their parents' wishes. If they do not want you to date yet, then you must adhere to their rules.

"Children, obey your parents in everything, for this pleases the Lord" (Colossians 3:20).

That said, let's look at what the Bible says about romantic relationships.

The Bible does not actually mention the words "dating" and "courtship," but we can definitely find some principles about relationships that will help us understand what's up with these touchy subjects. First things first, let's separate how the world views dating from how God wants us to handle the period of time before we get married.

According to 2 Peter 2:18-20, God's way is totally contradictory to the way the world says unmarried couples should act.

The World's View of Dating

When it comes to dating, the world constantly sends messages of try before you buy; dating as much as you want is totally fine, and sleeping around is necessary to see if you're physically compatible. The world also says living together before you're married is completely normal because, well, how else would you find out if your boyfriend's/girlfriend's habits are too annoying to live with?

Sadly, this is a very self-centered way of entering a relationship. This view is all about pleasing ourselves, not loving and serving another person. That kind of attitude and motivation will ultimately lead to a relationship ending in disaster. Even very well-meaning, God-loving Christian couples can fall into the trap of selfishness when it comes to relationships.

God's View of Dating

As said earlier, God's view of romance is quite different from the world's view. He wants us to first discover a person's innermost character, who he or she really is when no one is looking before we decide to make a commitment. When dating, you must think about the following:

- Does the person strengthen your relationship with Christ, or does he or she compromise your morals and standards?
- Has the person accepted Christ as his or her Savior (John 3:3-8; 2 Corinthians 6:14-15)?
- Is the person committed to becoming more like Jesus (Philippians 2:5) or does he or she live a selfish life?
- Does the person show love, joy, peace, patience, kindness, goodness, faithfulness, gentleness, and self-control, which are the fruit of the Spirit (Galatians 5:22-23)?

When you've committed to another person in a romantic relationship, remember to keep God as the most important person in your life (Matthew 10:37). You should never place anything or anyone before God because that is considered the sin of idolatry (Galatians 5:20; Colossians

3:5). This applies even if you mean well and love the person unconditionally. Strange as it sounds, having God as the focus of your life will help you to love that other person even better.

While dating or courting, be ever conscious of the need to avoid sexual temptation. It is not only a sin against God, but it is a sin against your body (1 Corinthians 6: 18). Respect yourself and the one you love by honoring him or her as Christ commands in Scripture. Set sexual boundaries for yourself. At the same time, observe if the person you are dating establishes similar limits or if he or she is willing to compromise.

"Love must be sincere. Hate what is evil; cling to what is good. Be devoted to one another in love. Honor one another above yourselves" (Romans 12:9-10).

Dating, courting, or whatever you want to call it can be a great way to solidify an already super-strong friendship and begin to build a solid foundation for marriage. If your parents have given their blessings, if God is at the center of your motivation, and you are both ready to step it up, then this could be a perfect time to move toward something more than "just friends." If you want to shoot for a lifelong, God-honoring union with your best friend, then that is when you know it's time to start a romance (Genesis 2:24; Matthew 19:5).

Your desire to be married is not ungodly, but the Devil intends to use it for bad purposes. It is his strategy to keep the divorce rates high and make marriage a battlefield.

That's why I am writing this book. I want you to know how to live according to the Word of God, not by the standards of this world. I want you to have a meaningful, God-sanctioned relationship that leads to a successful marriage. My heart breaks every time I receive calls from broken-hearted girls or boys crying because they were dumped after choosing to walk in ungodliness. They feel betrayed, stupid, and worthless and are left alone to deal with their wounds. Don't fall for the lies of the world. Sin destroys everything that is beautiful and exceptional. But true godliness produces joy in our lives and brings many blessings.

May God bless you abundantly as you continue reading this book. May the Holy Spirit give you strength to repair the areas of your life in which you are struggling.

CHAPTER TWO

WHY DO PEOPLE COURT?

"In those days Israel had no king; all the people did whatever seemed right in their own eyes" (Judges 17:6).

The above situation accurately describes today's culture. Youngsters and adults do as they please without any fear of God. You can choose to walk in the narrow way and submit to God's authority or to walk in the broader way which leads to hell. Mark my words, the choices you make when you are young will determine your future.

The first lie Satan told Adam and Eve is to live and learn. It is the same untruth that is popularly spread in our societies. We often hear from friends, family, the media, and others to live and learn. But God told Adam and Eve to do the opposite. He told them to learn and live. He warned them not to eat of the tree of good and evil. When God tells you something is good, it means it is good. You need to trust Him completely. But as Satan did with Adam and Eve, he comes along and whispers, "No, don't listen to God. Try it yourself. He doesn't want you to have fun." In other words, Satan wants us to live by the motto, "Live and Learn."

I encourage you to always listen to the voice of God and follow His will, not what you feel is right or what Satan whispers in your tingling ears.

"My people are being destroyed because they don't know me" (Hosea 4:6).

"Your word is a lamp to guide my feet and a light for my path" (Psalm 119:105).

Suppose you are lost in a big forest how will you find your way out? If you have a map, it will be very easy to get out but without it, you will be lost forever and eventually die. As the preceding Scripture verses show, God's Word functions in a similar way. It is the map of life. It gives us the directions we need to live successfully in this world. We need the Word of God to lead us in every aspect of our lives. His knowledge is essential to fulfilling our destinies. When knowledge decreases, ignorance increases.

"So whether you eat or drink, or whatever you do, do it all for the glory of God" (1 Corinthians 10:31).

If eating and drinking can glorify God, how much more should you glorify God with your marriage, life, work, and studies, etc.

If you are seeking to be with the opposite sex primarily for fun, not for the glory of God or to fulfill His purpose in marriage then you are just playing with your own life. In the long run, all you will be left with is an unrepairable life. Is that what you want? Of course not. You want happiness, peace, and love. So, you must ask yourself the pertinent question—why do you really want to court and have a romantic relationship?

Unfortunately, many people date with the sole intention of getting something from the opposite sex outside of the proper context of marriage. If you are doing this, it shows you don't have the backbone to take responsibility.

Furthermore, frankly speaking, if you are with someone just for your needs to be met, then it is not courting—it is prostitution. Are you with this person for your selfish dreams to come true or to use him or her to build your career?

Nothing is wrong with a young man desiring the fellowship of a young woman or vice versa. That is a wonderful thing. In fact, it is a God-given desire, but to enjoy it outside the confines of marriage in the wrong way is a sin. If you have already done it, this is the right time to get on your knees and ask for forgiveness.

You cannot enter a relationship with a shopper's mentality. Shoppers test-drive many models before they find the car they want to buy. This test-driving mindset is ungodly. Your body is God's temple. It was not made to be used and abused by anyone. For that matter, sex is not just a physical act; it is you giving body and soul to someone else. You cannot enter a sexual relationship without gaining or losing something, without a part of you being in that person forever and a part of that person being in you.

It is true we all desire companionship. But with the right perspective, singleness can be an advantage. When you are single, use your singleness for God. Read the Word of God. Study it. Pray and serve God by helping those in need. Make your youth useful for the Lord. Do not pursue a relationship until you are in a season of life where you are ready to get married. When it is time to study, study well. When it is time to work, work hard. When it is time to marry, pursue it seriously. Do not pursue a serious relationship until you are ready. If you are an alcoholic or drug addict, you are definitely not ready for a serious relationship. If you are unhappy with yourself, have not gotten over your past, or do not want to commit, you are not ready for a serious relationship.

Be reasonable about your expectations. Some people's expectations are ridiculous. I know Christians who have said no to good proposals just to marry NRIs and they are still unmarried. They are in their 40s now. What is the point I am making? Marry someone who loves you and accepts you gladly without any demands.

To be clear, going on a date with someone does not mean you're dating. Let me explain what I just said. Just because you have lunch, dinner, or coffee with someone you like does not qualify you as dating. And a date certainly does not end in bed. As I said earlier, if you not aiming for the ring then it is not a biblical courtship.

The man initiates; the woman responds. So guys must be prepared for a yes or no answer and not expect the girls to initiate. Girls, if a guy asks for your help in meeting a girl, then you should tell him to get on his bike and go home. Men must man up!

For your relationship to work properly, both of you must love God and put Him in front of you. Feel free to use technology wisely. To avoid temptation, do not meet each other alone; join others. Be careful and wise.

Only invest in a relationship with someone you are attracted to. Only marry a person who agrees with you on issues of gender and family. If you want your wife to be a homemaker but she wants to pursue her career, then it's not wise to marry. If you want a big family and she doesn't, then it's not wise to marry. Agreeing on the "big things" in life is very important. So, sisters, please sort out everything before, rather than regretting later. And brothers, learn to stand on your words. Do not show double standards.

Guard your heart. Do not give it to any roadside Romeo. Set standards for yourself. On your first date, do not start dreaming about how many kids you will have. Be careful.

"Guard your heart above all else, for it determines the course of your life" (Proverbs 4:23).

Create boundaries that only a wife or a husband should be able to cross. Why would anyone want to get married when he or she can get all the benefits minus the ring, the ceremony, and the paperwork? Men will give you false hope to get what they want. If you don't set any boundaries, you will be in deep trouble. Be prudent, my sister.

This chapter answered the question, "Why do people court?" Spend some time thinking about what you read and how you can apply it to your life.

CHAPTER THREE

What Should I Look for in a Wife?

1. A good wife must have personal faith and trust in the Lord Jesus

Personal faith and trust in the Lord Jesus is the basis for any and all other qualities on the list. It is hard to overstate the importance of ensuring we do not enter an intimate relationship with those who are not Christians. The Bible refers to this as being "unequally yoked" (2 Corinthians 6:14).

Paul commands believers to marry "only in the Lord" (1 Corinthians 7:39). A marriage in which only one partner is committed to godliness cannot be regarded as "in the Lord." Young men looking for wives must get the same warning as women searching for husbands. Christian men getting involved with non-Christian women is not as common as Christian women in relationships with non-Christian men. However, sometimes Christian men find themselves in deep friendships with unbelieving women. Despite the counsel they receive to the contrary, they desperately want to believe they will win these women over to Christianity once they get married. More often than not, these women make little effort to pursue spiritual things once the rings are on their fingers. Consequently, the men are left to go to church and work on their spiritual lives alone or worse yet, to eventually stop trying altogether. At this stage, the Devil's plan prevails in making one more incomplete marriage.

2. A wife must possess inner beauty

Guys should not just marry women based on looks. The reality is outward appearances will fade away with time, but inner beauty will not. Don't get me wrong. I am not saying beautiful girls lack inner beauty. Rather, I am advising men not to marry women merely for their external beauty. A wise man looks for a woman whose beauty comes from time spent in front of the mirror of the Word of God.

3. A wife should be modest

If a woman dresses well and draws attention to her face, then that is true, modest beauty. If her dress attracts all the attention to her body, then run away from her as if she has leprosy. She will never be satisfied with your attention. Why? Because any woman who dresses immodestly shows she seeks and loves attention from all men.

4. A wife should be able to handle stress well

All the decisions that come with marriage—having kids, making life-altering financial decisions, or business planning—are extremely stressful. Look for a woman who can work through those hard decisions with dignity and grace. Look for a woman who may get upset, raise her voice, and challenge you but who will also take a deep breath, hold your hand, and move forward with you after you've made the decision together.

5. A wife should be an initiative taker with an attitude of submission

The word submission is so frequently misunderstood it has become a sensitive issue for many people. God's intended role for the wife is not to wait around for her husband's directives as if she is somehow paralyzed without them. She is God's gift to man as a companion and helper. There will seldom be a day when a man who has a good wife does not have occasion to thank God for her wisdom and grace.

Having said that, however, you must not fall to the contrary. Desperately avoid self-opinionated women who are clearly unprepared to submit their hearts, minds, and lifestyles to the clear teaching of God's Word.

6. A good wife is not a nagger

It is hard to live with a woman who is continuously nagging for each and everything. If she has a nagging heart rather than a heart of gratitude, life is better without her (Proverbs 27:15, 25:24).

7. A good wife will not hurt her man's ego

Ego is a God-given gift to man for his masculinity. If a woman uses her wealth, education, or beauty to hurt a man's ego, she is not a good match for you.

8. A wife's behavior should build her husband's confidence

When a wife uses her tongue to speak words of wisdom and encouragement to her husband in hard times rather than nagging, she proves herself to be the perfect woman. It is much easier to put complete trust and confidence in such a person.

9. A wife should be prayerful

The power a praying wife possesses is not a means of gaining control over her husband. In fact, it is quite the opposite. When you pray, you put aside all claims to power in and of yourself and rely on God's power to transform you, your husband, your circumstances, and your marriage.

Men should diligently seek the qualities covered in this chapter when looking for a wife. However, there are many other qualities women should possess that are equally important. A woman who honors God and her husband by submitting to him shows the signs of being a godly woman. If you find one, don't lose her.

I hope this chapter has enriched you in some way. Brother in Christ, pray diligently before you choose your wife.

CHAPTER FOUR

What Should I Look for in a Husband?

Sister, keep one thing in mind: marriage is for men, not for boys.

1. A good husband must have personal faith and trust in the Lord Jesus

As said in the previous chapter, personal faith and trust in Jesus is the basis for any and all other qualities on the list. It is hard to overstate the importance of ensuring we do not enter intimate relationships with non-Christians. The Bible refers to this as being "unequally yoked" (2 Corinthians 6:14).

Paul commands believers to marry "only in the Lord" (1 Corinthians 7:39). A marriage in which only one partner is committed to godliness cannot be regarded as "in the Lord." Young men looking for wives must get the same warning as women searching for husbands. Christian men getting involved with non-Christian women is not as common as Christian women in relationships with non-Christian men.

However, sometimes Christian men find themselves in deep friendships with unbelieving women. Despite the counsel they receive to the contrary, they desperately want to believe they will win these women over to Christianity once they get married. More often than not, these women make little effort to pursue spiritual things once the rings are on their fingers. Consequently, the men are left to go to church and work on their spiritual lives alone or worse yet, to eventually stop trying altogether. At this stage, The Devil's plan prevails in making one more incomplete marriage.

2. A good husband will have a plan and vision for his future

"Then the LORD God said, "It is not good for the man to be alone. I will make a helper who is just right for him" (Genesis 2:18).

If a man approaches you with his vision and it resonates with you, meaning you think you want to join him in his venture, then you can say yes to him. However, do not entertain men who have no plans or ambitions. A man who does not have a plan for his life is a person going to battle without any armor. Women have a right to decide if they want to participate or not.

When I met my wife, I was absolutely clear to her that I was into full time ministry. I told her I did not have my own house, a government job, or a car. I was completely honest with her. Then I asked her if she wanted to be a part of my life, and she said yes after thinking about it. She believed in my vision. Today, she stands as a strong backbone of the vision God gave me.

This doesn't mean God cannot give my wife visions. In fact, he has already given her a vision for her life, and I am supporting her in accomplishing it. We are a team for the Lord, standing with each other for the expansion of God's kingdom.

3. A good husband will be tough in tough times

A man who is scared to face life, or who cannot stand in hard situations is not good enough to be a husband or a father. If you must force him to read the Bible, go to work or be active in church, then he cannot be a good husband, father, or Christian.

4. A good husband will be understanding, caring, and kind

When a man is courting, he is on his best behavior. Chances are his behavior will change as he becomes more comfortable with you. Be very careful and watch for red flags in his actions and attitudes. If he abuses you verbally, physically, or otherwise, then he is not the right man for you to marry. Do not fool yourself into thinking marriage will change him. In fact, he may get worse. Has he forced himself upon you? Does he respect your feelings? Do you feel safe or insecure around him? These are questions that must be answered before committing to him.

Intimacy in a relationship is about trust and trust is about safety, protection, shelter, and well-being. It is unpardonable if he beats you, shouts at you, or yells at you, even if you provoked him. A good husband will put himself in your situation and try to understand the trauma you are going through.

5. A good husband wants to be a father

There are three types of men:

1. Men who don't want kids
2. Men who want kids and expect the mother to raise them
3. Men who really want to be fathers

It is a father's responsibility to teach kids and his wife, not youth groups and Sunday school.

And you must love the LORD, your God with all your heart, all your soul, and all your strength. And you must commit yourselves wholeheartedly to these commands that I am giving you today. Repeat them again and again to your children. Talk about them when you are at home and when you are on the road, when you are going to bed and when you are getting up. Tie them to your hands and wear them on your forehead as reminders. Write them on the doorposts of your house and on your gates. (Deuteronomy 6:5-9)

"Direct your children onto the right path, and when they are older, they will not leave it" (Proverbs 22:6).

6. A good husband will be a one-woman man

"So an elder must be a man whose life is above reproach. He must be faithful to his wife" (1 Timothy 3:2).

If a man is addicted to porn, he is not a one-woman man. If he is sexually involved with two or three women at a time, he is not a one-woman man. If you are having lunch or dinner with him and he looks back at every girl who passes by, he is not a one-woman man. If a man cheats on you when you are dating him, he is not a one-woman man. Do not ignore the red flags. As Maya Angelou said, "When someone shows you who they are, believe them the first time."

You need a man like Job who said, "I made a covenant with my eyes not to look with lust at a young woman" (Job

31:1). Court a man who loves, desires, and pursues you, a man who will be attracted to you all the days of his life.

Girls should not try to compete with other girls. Comparison leads to discontentment, jealousy, and insecurity. You might try to look sexier and more attractive so he will love you more, but what if he doesn't? What if he finds someone else more appealing? You are not the problem. The problem is in his heart. Don't sin to try to get his attention and attract him to you. If you must do that to win him over, he is a boy, not a man. He is not a one-woman man.

7. A good husband will value you

If he is not willing to go to school, finish his college education, get a job, and stand on his feet, then he doesn't value you. A man who values you will be willing to attend church on his own, read the Bible on his own, and serve the Lord on his own.

Sister, do not make it easy for him to get you, make him earn it. Choose a man you would want your sons to be like, someone you would want your daughters to marry.

8. A good husband is committed to the kingdom of God

Lastly, a good husband will be committed to building the kingdom of God. He will put others before himself. He will be faithful in prayers. He will be connected to his family and others in the body of Christ.

I hope this chapter has challenged you not to undervalue yourself. Let any man or woman who wants you show it by his or her actions. I pray you will choose the right person for your life.

CHAPTER FIVE

HOW TO PREPARE FOR MARRIAGE

1. Develop a deeper relationship with God

Developing a closer relationship with God is an admirable goal. It reflects a heart that is truly reborn, for only those who are in Christ desire a closer relationship with God. We must also understand in this life, we will never be as close to God as we ought or desire to be.

You can have a closer relationship with God through the daily habit of confessing sins to Him, listening when He speaks, speaking to Him through prayer, finding a body of believers with whom you can regularly worship, and living in obedience.

2. Save money

We are accountable to God for how we use everything He gives us in this life, including money. Saving money demonstrates good stewardship of the resources God gives us. Saving money allows us to be prepared for the future and being prepared for the future is good.

3. Decrease debt

The Bible does not explicitly command against all forms of debt. Indeed, the Bible warns against debt and extols the virtue of not going into it, but it does not forbid debt. The wisdom of the Bible teaches us it is usually not a good idea to be indebted. Debt essentially makes us a slave to the one who provides the loan.

4. Pick up some extra skills

Everyone can use some extra cash at some point in life. Your choices and successes are up to you. Thankfully, you can do a lot of that work in your spare time.

5. Plan for your marriage

Make plans to do things that are not just profitable to yourself but to your marriage. God is the creator of marriage. It was His idea from the very beginning. God created marriage with something far more wonderful in mind than simply being a place where we can get our needs met and find happiness. God uses marriage to accomplish a very important goal: to help us become like Christ.

6. Seek wise counsel

Seek wisdom about marriage from people who know what they are talking about. Don't assume you know what you are doing.

Warning: Do not have any kind of sexual contact before marriage. In God's family, there shouldn't be any hint of sexual immorality.

"Let there be no sexual immorality, impurity, or greed among you. Such sins have no place among God's people" (Ephesians 5:3).

Learn to love God first. Being single with God is learning to become one with Him. This is essentially how marriage functions.

"The two shall become one single flesh" (Ephesians 5:31).

Marriage is not about the wedding; it is about what happens after. The person who you will marry will complement you in what God has called you to do and help you, but that doesn't mean he or she will be perfect. Always remember, marriage should not hinder you from carrying out the Great Commission.

CHAPTER SIX

INSPIRED MESSAGE

I strongly believe this small book has blessed you immensely and as a result, you are better equipped to choose a better partner. Do not follow what other people tell you to do; follow the Word of God. Whether you are married or unmarried, once you allow the Holy Spirit to work in your life, the following message will bless you immensely.

As I said at the beginning of this book, before God established the church on the earth, He instituted marriage. Marriage is one of the most sacred institutions created by God Himself. When two people are joined in holy matrimony, they become joint-heirs of God's gift of life.

In the Scriptures below, apostle Peter outlines how husbands and wives should live to maintain successful marriages:

Wives

In the same way, you wives must accept the authority of your husbands. Then, even if some refuse to obey the Good News. your godly lives will speak to them without any words. They will be won over by observing your pure and reverent lives.

Don't be concerned about the outward beauty of fancy hairstyles. expensive jewellery, or beautiful clothes. You should clothe yourselves instead with the beauty that comes from within, the unfading beauty of a gentle and quiet spirit, which is so precious to God. This is how the holy women of old made themselves beautiful. They trusted God and accepted the authority of their husbands. For instance, Sarah obeyed her husband, Abraham, and called him her master. You are her daughters when you do what is right without fear of what your husbands might do. (1 Peter 3:1-6)

Husbands

"In the same way, you husbands must give honor to your wives. Treat your wife with understanding as you live together. She may be weaker than you are, but she is your equal partner in God's gift of new life. Treat her as you should so your prayers will not be hindered" (1 Peter 3:1-7).

In 1 Peter 2:13-35, apostle Peter had already talked about submission. He outlined how citizens ought to submit to governing authorities and the way employees should submit to their employers.

From 1 Peter 2:13 to the end of the book, the real mega theme is submission to authority with various applications. Proceeding to 1 Peter Chapter 5, the author teaches that elders and pastors in the church should submit to Jesus.

In the middle of his discussions about submission in the church, at work, and to government, he also addresses the issue of submission as it pertains to the home (1 Peter 3:1-7).

When we explore Genesis Chapter 2, we see that God's ultimate intention was for the husband and wife to be one as God is one. However, the world has tarnished God's designs, and many have strayed from His divine plan. Nevertheless, God's plan for marriage remains the same.

A Christian marriage should have the following characteristics:

1. God is Lord over all

2. Man is the head and leader of the home (Colossians 3; 1 Peter Chapter 3; Ephesians Chapter 5)

He must love as Christ loves the church (Ephesians 5: 25).

3. The wife is to respect and follow the leadership of her husband (Colossians Chapter 3; 1 Peter Chapter 3; Ephesians Chapter 5).

4. Children ought to follow the leadership of their fathers and mothers. This is one of the Ten Commandments Paul echoes in Ephesians Chapter 6.

In a marriage, the husband is not the higher authority, God is. Moreover, governments and the church are also authorities over the husband. Therefore, if the husband is living in sin, his wife and kids don't have to live a painful life under him. They can appeal to the higher authority of God. The wife can call the elders and let them know what is happening. These elders are responsible for disciplining the husband. Alternatively, the wife can utilize the authority of the State and contact the police.

"Likewise, you wives, be in subjection to your own husbands" (1 Peter 3:1).

The preceding verse says wives must submit to their own husbands. Note carefully it does not say submit to men. It says submit to your own husband. We are talking about one woman submitting to one man. When you say, "I do" to each other, you say no to every other man and woman in your life, including your father and mother.

"That, if any obey not the word, they also may without the word be won by the conduct of the wives; 2 While they behold your chaste behaviour coupled with fear" (1 Peter 3: 1b).

Wives must understand God has given men egos for their manhood, so they should never try to become nagging women or to hurt their husbands' egos.

"Whose adorning let it not be that outward adorning of braiding the hair, and of wearing of gold, or of putting on of apparel; 4 But let it be the hidden man of the heart, in that which is not corruptible, even the ornament of a meek and quiet spirit, which is in the sight of God of great price" (1 Peter 3:3).

Nothing is wrong with wearing makeup, going to a spa, and maintaining yourself. I am a health freak. I am very conscious about my physique and health. But I do not overdo it. My focus is to live better, not only look better. I encourage you to do the same.

"For after this manner in former times the holy women also, who trusted in God, adorned themselves, being in subjection unto their own husbands: Even as Sara obeyed Abraham, calling him lord: whose daughters you are" (1 Peter 3:5-6).

God didn't choose Sarah because she was perfect. In fact, she wasn't perfect. And you won't be perfect either. So, don't expect to be.

- You won't be a perfect wife. Sarah wasn't.
- You may not give good counsel. Sarah didn't.
- You may not believe what God tells you. Sarah didn't.

"As long as you do well, and are not afraid of any terror" (1 Peter 3:6b).

As long as you trust in the Lord, life will go well for you. But if you fear your life will be miserable under your husband's leadership, don't live in fear; live by faith.

What Submission Does Not Mean

1. Husbands are the ultimate authority

Your husband is not the ultimate authority, he is accountable to God, the church, and government.

2. Wives should not seek to influence their husbands

Submission does not mean a woman has no say or influence in her relationship.

- Wives are helpers (Genesis 2:18).
- Prudent wives are from the Lord (Proverbs 19:14).

3. Wives must obey their husbands' commands to sin

God is the ultimate authority. In the final analysis, He is the one we should obey. If husbands follow Jesus, their wives will have no problems following them.

5. Wives are less intelligent than their husbands

Submission does not mean wives are less intelligent than their husbands. We are not talking about IQ. The husband as the leader of the household is responsible for the wellbeing of his wife and children.

What Submission Means

1. Husbands and wives are equal and have complementary roles.

The higher the authority, the bigger the responsibility.

2. Wives are to submit as Jesus did in Gethsemane.

3. Husbands are to lovingly lead their wives as Jesus does the church.

4. A single woman should only marry a man she can follow.

5. Christian marriage reflects the Trinity and gospel.

Jesus died for our sins even though He was sinless. Likewise, husbands should love their wives to the point where they are willing to lay down their lives for them.

Marriage is a covenant. In every covenant, a head is appointed to oversee the covenant.

6. A wife is not less intelligent than him in the members of the covenant or cared for - (Malachi 2: 14, Proverbs 2:17).

Within marriage, the covenant head is the man. That's why in the New Testament, you will continuously read that man is the head, but that doesn't mean he is better than the woman.

God holds men and women responsible for their sins, but He puts an additional burden on the man for the wellbeing of his family. That's why God asked Adam, "Where are you?" (Genesis 3:9).

"Likewise, you husbands, dwell with them according to knowledge, giving honor unto the wife, as unto the weaker vessel, and as being heirs together of the grace of life; that your prayers be not hindered" (1 Peter 3:7).

How Men Should Treat Their Wives

1. You should love her martially

"Husbands, love your wives, even as Christ also loved the church, and gave himself for it" (Ephesians 5:25).

2. Honor her physically

"Women are the weaker vessel" (1 Peter 3:7).

3. Honor her emotionally

"Adam was with her and he knew her, share every day with each other" (Genesis 4:1).

4. Honor her verbally

Children will pick up how husbands speak with their wives.

5. Honor her financially

Men who don't provide the needs of their families have denied the faith and are worse than unbelievers.

6. Honor her practically

Show love, care, and support by your actions, not just mere words.

7. Honor her parentally

Husbands are also like fathers to their wives. They are to correct, guide, and love them unconditionally.

8. Honor her spiritually

It is a man's job to lead his family spiritually. Husbands are to read the Bible. They are the ones to lead the family to church and initiate prayer with the wife.

What happens to a guy who doesn't do what Peter said?

"That your prayers be not hindered" (1 Peter 3: 7 b)

Men who fail to honor their wives will have their prayers hindered. Know one thing very clearly, before a Christian sister is a daughter of an earthly man, she is God's daughter. If you mess with God's daughter, He will not answer your prayers. If you keep God's daughter safe and sound with love and care, He will answer all your prayers.

What Is the Purpose of Marriage?

Marriage is meant to conform us to the image of Jesus Christ.

"For whom he did foreknow, he also did predestine to be conformed to the image of his Son, that he might be the firstborn among many brethren" (Romans 8:29).

God conforms us through scriptures, prayers, and problems, but one of the main ways of being conformed to the image of Christ is marriage.

In the process of taking your family to church, God is working through His Spirit and His words to change you. God will use your spouse to help you conform to the image of God. He may give you a partner who is weak in an area you hoped he or she would be strong in. This will strengthen your muscles of patience and prayer.

You might be wondering why God created marriage if it is imperfect. The answer is God designed marriage to conform us into the image of Christ. Always remember, the obstacles and difficulties in marriage produce the greatest conformity to Christ in our lives.

I suggest you take one day at a time. Do not think you have to live with him or her for the next 50 years. Remember you are living on borrowed time. Love each other as if this is your last night together.

At this point, I believe you have learned at least one thing from this book. If the Lord delays His coming, we will meet. Before I leave, I would like to pray for you:

Father, in the name of Jesus, we come to Your throne of grace. I give Your sons and daughters in Your loving and gracious hands. Be with them and help them to make the right decisions for their lives. Thank You for leading them. In Jesus' precious name, we pray. Amen! Amen! Amen!

Stay blessed!

Shalom!

In His firm grip,

Evans Francis

About The Author

Evans Francis's life story is an inspiration for all young people who are growing up in a world that does not always seem conducive to faith.

Nagpur is a large city in central India, famous for its sumptuous oranges, delightful cultural events, and literature. The Orange City, as it is famously called, is home to a large number of Hindus and a considerable population of Buddhists and Muslims. However, the Christian community represents just a meager 1.15 % of the over 2.4 million people.

It would be easy to think that a Christian in Nagpur who is determined to share their faith and spread the word of God would struggle, be discouraged, and feel like a lonely voice in the wilderness. For many Christians, that may well be the case—but not for 33-year-old Evans Francis, who is bringing people to Christ by the thousands with his ministry.

In a world where the faith of the Christian community is being challenged and undermined by a growing number of people who are becoming atheists, Evangelist Evans Francis has shown that it is possible for Christians to be relevant, compassionate, and uncompromising in their faithfulness towards the Holy Scriptures.

Who is Evangelist Evans Francis?

Born in the modest Indian village of Mukerian, Punjab, in 1988, Evans began his evangelistic career at the very tender age of 19. On answering the call from God, he put everything behind and began a journey in the service of the

Lord, which has taken him all over India and different parts of the world.

Despite many challenges and obstacles, Evans did not deviate from his work but continued to follow the vision and calling of God upon his life.

Early struggles with life-threatening ailments

Evan's life has not been an easy one, even as a baby. At just six months old, he was already battling epilepsy, which everyone, including medical experts, concluded would be a lifelong struggle. But, Evans remarks that a greater authority had different plans for his life.

"When I was six months old, I underwent treatment for epilepsy. I was treated in Christian Medical College in Ludhiana. I used to get electric shocks—doctors said I would be like this throughout my life. But today, I'm a postgraduate. What is impossible for man is possible for God."

This marked his first victory in his life, one which he attributes to the grace of God. However, there was more to come. As a freshman in high school, Evans faced yet another health issue—he was diagnosed with Acute Pancreatitis. This is a condition where the pancreas becomes inflamed or swollen over a short period of time.

What was really surprising about this ailment is that it is very rare among kids. In fact, it occurs in one in a million among children. So why was Evans so unlucky? Life at this point seemed hell on earth for him—each day was a struggle to survive, as he was in agonizing pain, vomiting, and completely bedridden.

To make matters worse, Evans couldn't seek immediate treatment due to the dire financial situation of his family. A life-threatening disease that should have been attended to immediately was delayed for three whole days. But against all odds, he defied medical science and pulled through, yet again.

"When I was in 9th Standard, I suffered from a disease called Acute Pancreatitis. During the time, I used to vomit 50 times a day. When I was taken to the hospital after three days, I was in agonizing pain. The Doctors said I might not survive because it took three days for me to reach the hospital due to our financial condition. But in 7 days, I got discharged supernaturally. Again I say, what is impossible for man is possible for God."

For someone so young, Evans had already experienced two major health issues—a rare one, at that. What was even more surprising was the way he was able to recover and defeat the odds twice. It felt like God was giving him a second chance to live, this time with good health.

Unfortunately, the celebration was short-lived. Once again, Evans had another health problem—this time, it was his Kidney. Why was such a young boy constantly haunted by health issues?

His family was left in despair after it was confirmed in a hospital that he was suffering from Kidney Stones. The sonography was clear as day; Evans needed to undergo a medical procedure if he wanted to survive this storm.

Interestingly, rather than opt for immediate treatment, Evans and his family resorted to prayers. It seemed like a tall order for a young boy to get divine intervention, but his faith in the Lord was unwavering. With faith, he went with his family to another diagnostic center, and his results returned normal—the stone was nowhere to be found.

"There was a time a Doctor had told me that I have Kidney Stones, and sonography confirmed that. We prayed and went to another diagnostic center; believe it or not, the stone was not there. I believe that Jesus has healed me," he said.

Evans explained that the consistent health problems he faced in his early life, and even the gruesome car accident he experienced, once led him to believe that he was cursed. There was no rhyme or reason to it—he could not understand why God would choose him for such suffering.

In his words, "I have gone through thousands of injections in my life; I used to see myself as the cursed one. But now I understand that all things work together for good, for those who love God."

Building on victories

The complete restoration of health gave Evans a new lease on life, and he feels like God has given him a special gift in his hands—a chance to serve humanity by testifying about how they can also be healed completely through faith in God's promises.

Evans, who has been a victor in all his battles up to this point which would have broken the spirit of many people, wants every Christian to know that God is on their side. In fact, he quotes a scripture in the Bible (Psalm 118:17) which says, "I shall not die, but live: and shall declare the works of the Lord."

On 18 July 2017, Evans married Neha, who was born and brought up in Bhilai, Chattisgarh, and together they are fulfilling their mission and travel around the globe.

Spreading the word

Evans has established churches, teaches and preaches the Word of God, and is busy leading many to the Kingdom of God. In addition, he has authored a number of Christian books and composed several beautiful songs that have touched lives among listeners worldwide.

This visionary evangelist is also maximizing digital media to spread the gospel, one of which is his YouTube channel, "Evans Francis," with millions of views to date. He fearlessly shares the dreams, visions, and messages that God gives him for the body of Christ, which are posted on his mobile app "Evans Francis," available on Google Play and Apple Store for free.

As is evident, Evans has had to go through life-threatening trials and tribulations. But nothing could hold him back from fulfilling his calling—which is to reach out with the love of God to as many people in the world as possible.

www.ingramcontent.com/pod-product-compliance
Lightning Source LLC
Chambersburg PA
CBHW020517160726
47991CB00007B/2988